Foreword by
Sam Silverstein
Author of *No More Excuses*

POWER

OF

INFLUENCE

INCREASE YOUR INCOME AND PERSONAL IMPACT

TY BENNETT

The Power of Influence
Sound Concepts, Inc.
782 S Auto Mall Dr., Suite A
American Fork, Utah 84003

For additional copies of this book please visit
www.increaseinfluence.com or www.SoundConcepts.com

No information contained herein is meant to replace the advice of a doctor or healthcare practitioner. The data and opinions appearing in this book are for informational purposes only. Readers are encouraged to seek advice from qualified health professionals.

ISBN 978-1-933057-72-9

Advanced Praise for The Power of Influence

"Big ideas can come in small packages, and this gem by Ty Bennett shines. Frank, authoritative, and informative, The Power of Influence compiles some of the best examples of influence available from today's greatest leaders."

- **Stephen M. R. Covey,** Author of the New York Times Bestseller *The Speed of Trust*

"Like other greats before it - The Compound Effect by Darren Hardy, The Success Principles by Jack Canfield... The Power of Influence is in a special category of books you should read year after year for the succinct wisdom and timeless lessons about becoming a person of influence."

- **Andrea Waltz,** Co-author of *Go for No!*

"There is a reason why Ty Bennett is super successful and his recipe is revealed in his new book 'The Power of Influence.' His easy to understand way of sharing his stories and the stories of the ultra successful will give you the power to influence."

- **Louis Lautman,** Founder of The Young Entrepreneur Society

"The Power of Influence is How To Win Friends & Influence People for our day."

- **Peter Vidmar,** Olympic Gold Medalist

"This book is a MUST READ for all who are yearning to enlighten their own destiny. Ty Bennett masterfully scribes, in detail, that the power of INFLUENCE in one's life is directly entwined with personal happiness, progress, and prosperity!"

- **Chad Hymas,** Bestselling Author, Speaker, and Wheel chair World Record Holder

"The Power of Influence shares simple truths sprinkled with practical, real-world insights that demystify the notion of how to make a BIG, positive difference in our work, our community and our family."

- **Kevin Carroll,** Author and Katalyst

"The short-sighted employ manipulation, coercion and force to get others to do it their way. They are takers. A real leader serves, inspires and supports others. They are givers. The Power of Influence teaches us how we can become givers yet get all that we ever wanted. Ty does it again!!"

- **Dave Blanchard,** CEO of The Og Mandino Group

"Influence is one of the major keys to success. If you want to be more successful and influential - you need to read this book!"

- **TJ Hoisington,** Bestselling Author of *If You Think You Can!*

"The Power of Influence will enhance your leadership, expand your business, and make your personal relationships more rewarding!"

- **Mike Robbins,** Author of *Be Yourself, Everyone Else is Already Taken*

"Whatever your destination, the simple, wise and insightful message from The Power of Influence will ripple out into every aspect of your life, transforming the journey towards success, joy and purpose."

- **Alexandra Delis-Abrams,** Ph.D., Author of *Attitudes, Beliefs and Choices*

Acknowledgements

It's funny, writing a book about influence and realizing the profound influence that so many people have had on my life and this message. There are many people who I need to thank.

It was Bob Burg and John David Mann who inspired me to write this book. Their runaway bestseller, The Go-Giver is the catalyst behind the message and one of my all time favorite books. Thanks guys!

Lee Benson, who is as great a guy as he is a writer. Lee, thank you for your amazing efficiency and for making the words sing.

A big thank you to Kyle Clouse and Caroline Rodgers who came up with the title. Great work!

There are many close friends and family who were early readers and gave me tremendous feedback and advice: Hyrum Knapp, Amber Robbins, Kip Enger, Jackie Fagerstrom, Ryan Peterson, Jesse Allen, Tim & Sally Bennett.

Nate Cox and the group at Sound Concepts, as well as Chad Lanenga for their amazing design skills. Thank you for making this happen.

And as always, thank you to my wonderful wife Sarah for her constant support, incredible enthusiasm and positive influence.

CONTENTS

Dedicated to all of the people who use
their influence to make a difference.

FOREWORD

John Maxwell said, "Leadership is influence." But here is a secret – sales is influence, parenting is influence, teaching is influence, and politics is influence. The power to influence is essential in every industry, position, situation and station in life.

Influence is all about the capacity to have an effect on someone or something. Influence allows you to drive action in your family, your business and your community. So what drives influence? Accountability.

The most powerful attribute of any leader is accountability. While many people see accountability as standing up and taking the responsibility when something goes wrong, the truth is that the leader who has created real influence understands that accountability is proactive, is omnipresent and always beyond compromise.

On your journey to build greater influence in your life and expand your sphere of influence, accountability should be at the very vortex. When you understand and live a life based in accountability you will discover that people are naturally attracted to you and your causes. People value the opinion of highly accountable people and that leads directly to influence.

Many times people try and put themselves in a position of influence. They feel it comes from job title or position. The truth is that the most powerful forms of influence, like respect, are earned. Your actions tell a story that the people around you absorb and respond to. It is your accountability that infiltrates your story. When you think about the most effective leaders of our time you will find that accountability is at their very core and that their influence emanates from that core.

People are influenced by individuals who they respect. When we look up to someone we value their thoughts, opinions and the way they do things. Think about great people of accountability and influence; Mahatma Gandhi, Abraham Lincoln, Nelson Mandela, Mother Teresa, and Martin Luther King, Jr. People around the world strive to be like them, talk like them, share insights and wisdom like them and do important things like them. These individuals inspire millions to be better, do more and make a difference. All of these individuals understood the importance of accountability, knew what their beliefs were and held themselves accountable to those beliefs and the people around them. Serving people was at their very core.

Influence is greatly impacted by the way you treat and engage with people. The most accountable people I know are always more concerned about the people around them then themselves. When the perception is that you are more concerned with others, then other people trust, respect and listen to what you have to say. Contributing to someone's success creates influence.

In The Power of Influence you are going to learn exactly how to address influence and leverage it for personal and organizational growth. You will learn specifically what you are accountable for and to do in order to enhance your personal influence. The insights and techniques that Ty Bennett shares with you will turn on your brain and engage your heart so you can channel your thoughts and actions and ultimately become a person of immense personal influence.

Sam Silverstein
Author: "No More Excuses"
Founder: The Accountability Academy

INTRODUCTION

As the New Year approaches I enjoy spending time reviewing my goals and my progress from the previous twelve months and setting goals for the next. I look at my life in four parts: Physical, mental, emotional & spiritual. I set goals in each. I think about what I want to be in each category, why I want it and how I am going to achieve it. It is one of my favorite times of the year.

Four years ago, I added something different to my goal setting session. I decided to choose a word: one single word that I would focus on throughout the year. It became the subject of my study, the focus of my thoughts, and it defined the trait I wished to gain in that year. Like Benjamin Franklin's 13 virtues, my word would become part of me in that year.

Four years ago I chose the word communication. I always felt like I was a natural communicator but I wanted to turn a raw talent into a strength. At the time I wanted to become a professional speaker and was speaking regularly in building our business. I read books on communication, presenting, public speaking and story telling. I worked very hard to eliminate any filler words from my speech, such as um, or ah. I recorded myself every time I presented, either in audio or video, and analyzed what worked, what didn't work, and how I might improve. That year my communication vastly improved and is something I continue to work on today.

Three years ago I chose the word Leader. I read every book I could get my hands on about leadership. "The 21 Irrefutable Laws of Leadership" by John Maxwell, "The 7 Habits of Highly Effective People" by Stephen Covey and "The Success Principles" by Jack Canfield were my favorites. I learned that leadership is an attitude and that you can and should lead regardless of your title, position, or role in life. John Quincy Adams said, "If your actions inspire others to dream more, learn more, do more and become more, you are a leader." From my friend Kevin Hall, author of "Aspire!," I learned that the word leader means Pathfinder. Someone who has found his or her path and lives on purpose is a leader and I strive to do that every day.

Two years ago I chose the word Humility. Often called the mother of all virtues, humility is having the disposition to always be learning and growing. It is being open and willing to develop new skills, gain new vantage points and become more. It is learning to not take yourself too seriously (I'm still working on that) and being open to feedback. It is interesting because as I sought to learn humility, I experienced many false starts, setbacks and failures that year. It is like someone was trying to teach me humility through experiential learning. Humility is definitely a lifelong pursuit.

At the beginning of this year, I wanted a word that applied to all my roles. In all of my personal relationships: as a husband, father, son, brother, grandson and friend. Professionally: as a speaker, author, entrepreneur, leader, salesman, marketer, teacher and mentor. As a neighbor in my community and as an involved participant in my church. In everything I did, I wanted a word that was relevant across the board, and the word is *Influence.*

THE PEOPLE BUSINESS

Chapter 1

THE PEOPLE BUSINESS

> "Dealing with people is probably the biggest problem you face, especially if you are in business. Yes, and that is also true if you are a housewife, architect or engineer"
> – Dale Carnegie

On a recent out-of-town trip, I checked into my hotel, where a friendly man wearing a big smile greeted me. As I was filling out the registration card, he asked a typical travel question: "Are you here for business or pleasure?"

I responded by saying, "Business."

Then he asked, "What business are you in?"

I thought about it for a second and said, "The same business as you – I'm in the people business."

Think about it. No matter what we do, where we go, or how we define ourselves, we're all in the people business.

We're in the people business at work, at home, in social settings and everywhere in between. The No. 1 key to your success in business and in life is your ability to relate to and get along with other people. Our ability to connect, interact, network, work with, persuade, listen to, engage, serve, pay attention to and get to know others – those are the factors that most determine and define our influence. That influence can go one-way – or the other.

Flying out of Salt Lake City, I almost always fly Delta. Because I fly with Delta so often, I am upgraded to first class virtually every time I fly. Not too long ago I was going to Oakland, California – a quick, painless flight – and I was upgraded to first class. I was the first one on the plane. I sat down in seat 4B, pulled out my iPad and was getting a few things done before takeoff.

As I was sitting there, looking down, all of a sudden a guy says, "You are in my seat. Get up." He said it just like that: "Get up!"

I looked up and said, "Wow, I'm sorry, what seat are you in?"

He said, "Do you realize this is first class, I'm sitting in first class and this is my seat." (Don't you love dealing with difficult people?) I said, "I know, I am in first class also – what is your seat?" Then he asked what I still view as the dumbest question I've ever been asked, "Did you pay to sit in first class or just get upgraded, because I paid for my seat." I replied, "Well that stinks. I was upgraded, which means I paid a lot less money for the exact same seat. What seat is yours?" "4C," he answered. I said, "Then that is your seat over there," and pointed to the other side of the aisle.

He simply turned and sat down in his seat, with no apology whatsoever. By then I couldn't help myself, so I said, "You know what, you would suck at what I do" He said, "Why is that?" And I said, "Because you are not good with people. In fact you are horrible with people. Just be nice. It's not that hard."

It was Mahatma Gandhi who said, "I suppose leadership at one time meant muscles; but today it means getting along with people."

HOWARD SCHULTZ

Personally, I am not a coffee drinker so I'm not much of a coffee connoisseur. But there is a phenomenon that exists in 50 countries around the world. The minute you think of coffee (myself included) there is only one name that comes to mind: Starbucks. With more than 17,000 stores, Starbucks Corporation is not only the largest coffeehouse company in the world, it is one of those rare companies that personify an industry.

Every phenomenon also carries with it an icon. Bill Gates of Microsoft, Steve Jobs of Apple, Phil Knight of Nike, Meg Whitman of eBay, Jeff Bezos of Amazon, Ray Kroc of McDonalds, Oprah of just, well, Oprah. In the case of Starbucks the icon is Howard Schultz.

Howard Schultz was born in 1952 and raised in a Brooklyn, N.Y., housing project. A football scholarship to Northern Michigan University was his ticket out, and after graduating he worked a variety of jobs until becoming manager of U.S. operations for a European house wares company called Hammarplast.

Schultz's adventure started in 1981 when he traveled from New York to Seattle to check out a popular coffee bean store called Starbucks that had been buying many of the Hammarplast Swedish drip coffeemakers he was selling. There was that great smell, sure, but what caused him to fall in love with the business was the care the Starbucks owners put into choosing and roasting the beans.

"I walked away ... saying, 'what a great company, what a great city. I'd love to be a part of that,'" Shultz said.

It took Schultz a year to convince the Starbucks owners to hire him. When they finally made him director of marketing and operations in 1982, he had another epiphany. This one occurred in Italy, when Schultz took note of the coffee bars that existed on practically every block. He learned that they not only served excellent espresso, they also served as meeting places or public squares; they were a big part of Italy's societal glue, and there were 200,000 of them in the country.

But back in Seattle, the Starbucks owners resisted Schultz's plans to expand to multiple stores, saying they didn't want to get into the restaurant business. Frustrated, Schultz quit and started his own coffee-bar business, called Il Giornale. It was successful, and a year later Schultz bought Starbucks for $3.8 million.

As Chairman and CEO of Starbucks today, Howard Schultz has continued to expand the Starbucks name and brand around the world. Although their coffee is top of the line (or so I'm told), Starbucks success goes way beyond coffee. Their trademark is friendly, trustworthy customer service. This is an idea reinforced constantly by Howard to his team as he states, "We are not in the coffee business serving people, we are in the people business serving coffee."

Regardless of what we do, whether we are in sales, HR, real estate, or retail. We all interact with people on a daily basis and as our ability to connect with people improves, we will be happier, healthier and wealthier.

WILT CHAMBERLAIN

"The most important single ingredient to the formula of success is knowing how to get along with people."
– Teddy Roosevelt

Wilt Chamberlain, the 7-foot professional basketball player, is considered one of the greatest and most dominant players to ever play in the National Basketball Association. In the late 1960s Wilt Chamberlain was traded to the Los Angeles Lakers. At the press conference that introduced him to local writers and broadcasters, a reporter asked, "Wilt, do you think Lakers' Coach Van Breda Kolff can handle you? It's been said that you are hard to handle."

Wilt responded, "You handle farm animals. You work with people. I am a person. I can work with anyone."

Wilt was right. We all work with people. We all engage in conversation, correspondence, argument, debate, and discussion. We all interact in business, civic, community, team and personal situations.

It doesn't matter your station in life, whether you're the CEO of the company or the new guy, we all have to learn to work with people.

John Craig said, "No matter how much work you can do, no matter how engaging your personality may be, you will not advance far in business if you cannot work with others."

I know we've all, at one time or another asked ourselves the following questions:

- Why do some people struggle in relationships while others flourish?
- Why do some people seem to have more influence and

do more business than others?

- Why do some leaders engender trust, respect, and loyalty from their people while others seem to only bring about distaste?
- Why do some people thrive in the people business while others dive?

SIX WAYS TO MAKE PEOPLE LIKE YOU

When it comes to books about networking, building relationships and working with people, the undisputed classic is "How To Win Friends and Influence People." Dale Carnegie wrote the book in 1936 and it has been read by millions of people since.

One of the great realizations in the book is that although some people are more extroverted or affable, working with people is a learned skill that anyone can master.

In the second section of the book, Carnegie offers what he calls "Six Ways To Make People Like You." These are simple suggestions that can make a huge difference in the way you work with people.

#1 – Be Genuinely Interested In Other People.

Studies show that the most frequently said word is "I." People love to talk about themselves, their lives, their hobbies, their families, their passions, etc. When you interact with people, ask questions and allow them to talk, they will love you for it.

#2 – Smile

A smile is a simple gesture that doesn't cost money, time, or energy but it can brighten someone's day; it changes the way you feel and makes you more approachable. Smiling is attractive and contagious. People around you can't help but smile when they see a big smile on your face.

#3 – Remembering and Using People's Name

They say that the sweetest and most important sound in language is the sound of your own name. In Jack Welch's book "Winning," when asked which restaurant was his favorite, he replied: "The one where they know my name." We've all been there: when you recognize someone but can't remember their name. It's awkward, uncomfortable and embarrassing. We often use the excuse that "I am not good with names," but if you want to master people, you need to begin to remember names. Develop a system. When you meet someone use their name three times in conversation or write their name down in a notebook with some details about them. Figure out a system that works for you.

#4 Be A Good Listener

As the sage saying goes, we were given one mouth and two ears for a reason. We need to encourage others to talk and then we need to listen to understand what they are saying. Listening is much more than being silent. It is an active process. It involves empathy -- the ability to walk in someone's shoes and understand them without judging or fixing. Listening is a skill that is developed with practice. As you master it, people will like you more and more.

#5 Talk To People In Terms of Their Interests

People love it when you can relate to their interests. Being knowledgeable on subjects they enjoy and capable of engaging in intelligent conversation about what matters most to them says volumes about your interest in who they are. That doesn't mean that you have to be an expert in every category, but being able to talk to people in terms of their interests goes a long way. One way to do this is to study topics of interest before meeting with people. If you know that your business lunch is with a huge baseball fan, then take some time to brush up on your knowledge of the game. This small point may make the biggest difference in how the lunch turns out. Talking in terms of other people's interests is another way to put them first and leave a great impression. If you have paid attention to the first five ways to make people like you, you are probably noticing a trend. Each of the points is focused on the other person.

#6 Make People Feel Important

Making people feel important can be done in a myriad of ways. You can give a compliment, remember their birthday or a special occasion, recognize them for their skills and contribution, or give them a gift. The key is to make sure you do it sincerely. Your motives must be pure. This is not about giving to get, it is about giving because you care. People read through individuals who are fake and only in it for themselves. If you are going to compliment someone, make it sincere. Look at the good in people and point that out. As a boy scout I was taught to leave a campsite better than I found it. I think the same principle applies to people. Leave every person better for having met you.

THE PEOPLE BUSINESS TODAY

As technology continues to shrink the planet we live on, the people business only continues to expand. Today we are more connected than anytime in history. Facebook, Twitter, Linked In, Skype, Myspace, Tumblr, and on and on -- they all make social networking truly worldwide. We can have a face-to-face conversation with someone half-a-world away, instantaneously. We send notes back and forth all day through text messages and email that used to take days. We've moved from living in the isolated country, to living in communities built around cities. More than ever, we are all connected. We are definitely all in the people business. We might as well get good at it.

WHAT DETERMINES YOUR INFLUENCE?

Chapter 2

WHAT DETERMINES YOUR INFLUENCE?

"No one can understand that mysterious thing we call influence ... yet ... everyone of us continually exerts influence, either to heal, to bless, to leave marks of beauty; or to wound, to hurt, to poison, to stain others lives."

– J. R. Miller

What is influence?

According to the dictionary, influence is "the power to sway or effect based on prestige, wealth, ability or position." That definition would seem to suggest that affluence determines influence.

And yet, one of the poorest women, in terms of financial wealth, the world has ever known was also one of the most influential: Mother Teresa.

In a life devoid of materialism, Mother Teresa spread her influence of love and selflessness around the world. It was her lack of position, as we normally think of it, which touched so many. As much as anything she did, it was her words that spread a legacy of love:

- "Every time you smile at someone, it is an action of love, a gift to that person, a beautiful thing."
- "In this life we cannot do great things. We can only do small things with great love.
- "One of the greatest diseases is to be nobody to anybody."
- "Even the rich are hungry for love, for being cared for, for being wanted"

When I think of the people who have had the most influence on me, their influence isn't based in what they have; it comes from who they are. A more all-encompassing definition of influence comes from Bob Burg and John David Mann in "The Go-Giver:" "Your influence is determined by how abundantly you place other people's interests first."

THE THREE TYPES OF INFLUENCE

> "There are no moral shortcuts in the game of business
> – or life. There are, basically, three kinds of people: the
> unsuccessful, the temporarily successful, and those
> who become and remain successful. The difference is
> character."
> – Jon Huntsman

hether it's at home, at work, at play, or anywhere in between, our influence on those around us will fall into three
categories:

Situational Influence – People follow you because they
have to. Position and authority most often determine this
kind of influence. A political leader, for example, or a CEO, or
a school teacher, or a traffic cop. This is the most common
type of influence, based on position, title and authority. It is
influence bequeathed, not personally earned, and exercis-
ing it can be done lazily because following is not a choice.
When people are forced or compelled to follow you in a
particular situation, the most you will ever get out of them is
compliance. And as Dondi Scumaci likes to say, "Compliance will never take you where commitment can go."

If you are an influencer who has a position of authority, step back and ask yourself this question:

Outside of this situation, do I still have influence over these people?

The answer will tell you what type of influence you hold.

Temporary Influence – People follow you because of what you've done. Maybe you just hit the game-winning home run, or you led the way out of a burning building. Or perhaps you have front row tickets for "Wicked." All of those are great things that attract attention and cause others to want to be involved, however peripherally, but to be truly influential we need to continue to perform at a high level or we will not continue to have strong influence.

An example of temporary influence would be a salesperson who gets a strong recommendation. The endorsement from a trusted source provides temporary influence with the potential client that opens the door. To turn that influence into a relationship, however, can't be based on past performance; it has to be based on current performance and results.

Lasting Influence – People follow because of who you are and how you treat them. Lasting influence is what every leader, salesperson, teacher, speaker, friend or mentor seeks. It is grounded in consistency of character. With this type of influence, no one is forced or compelled to follow you. Instead, they choose to follow you because they buy into you and find worth in your leadership. Regardless of the situation, there is influence. It is not situational and it is not temporary, because you continually provide value. Situational Influence and Temporary Influence can turn into Lasting Influence, but only when the important ingredient of integrity is permanently added.

Integrity is defined as wholeness, completeness; living a life of integrity means a life of honesty and honor. And therein lies the key to real influence. It was Ralph Waldo Emerson who said, "I cannot find language of sufficient energy to convey my sense of the sacredness of private integrity."

Warren Buffett put it another way: "I look for three things in hiring people. The first is personal integrity, the second is intelligence, and the third is a high energy level. But, if you don't have the first, the other two will kill you."

GANDHI

In the book, "The Speed of Trust," Stephen M. R. Covey uses the example of the great political and spiritual leader, Mahatma Gandhi, to illustrate lasting integrity.

"A great example of congruence is Mahatma Gandhi. At one point in his life, he was invited to speak before the House of Commons in England. Using no notes, he spoke for two hours and brought an essentially hostile audience to a rousing standing ovation. Following his speech, some reporters approached his secretary, Mahadev Desai, incredulous that Gandhi could mesmerize his audience for such a long period of time with no notes.

Desai responded, "What Gandhi thinks, what he feels, what he says, and what he does are all the same. He does not need notes … You and I, we think one thing, feel another, say a third, and do a fourth, so we need notes and files to keep track."

Gandhi is a supreme example of a person of influence. He not only changed a nation; his example, teachings and influence are still felt all around the world. Books have been written on Gandhi and his impeccable integrity, but for our purposes, let's look at seven investments he made in his integrity, that we can make in ours.

SEVEN INVESTMENTS IN INTEGRITY

1) Be The Same Person In Your Public, Private & Secret Life

> "My life is an indivisible whole, and all my activities run into one another ... my life is my message."
> – Mahatma Gandhi

All of us can think of examples of people we know who are one person in public and someone totally different in private. They portray a front, play a part, or put on a show for the world but that is not who they really are. Too many people harbor addictions, keep secrets, and think they can compartmentalize their life. Sooner or later it will catch up to them and their true self will be revealed.

Integrity is being whole or complete, which means you are who you are in every area of your life. Being the same person in your public life, private life and secret life creates transparency. Total freedom from worry, insecurity, and accusation. Take assessment of yourself. As you read this poem, analyze how you are doing with this investment.

Am I True to Myself

I have to live with myself, and so
I want to be fit for myself to know,
I want to be able, as days go by,
Always to look myself straight in the eye;
I don't want to stand, with the setting sun,
And hate myself for things I have done
I don't want to keep on a closet shelf
A lot of secrets about myself,
And fool myself as I come and go,
Into thinking that nobody else will know
The kind of man I really am;
I don't want to dress up myself in sham.
I want to go out with my head erect,
I want to deserve all men's respect;
But here in the struggle for fame and pelf
I want to be able to like myself.
I don't want to look at myself and know
That I'm bluster, bluff and empty show.
I can never hide myself from me;
I see what others may never see;
I know what others may never know,

I never can fool myself, and so,
Whatever happens, I want to be
Self-respecting and conscience free.

– Edgar Guest

2) Take Responsibility

> "Be The Change You Wish To See In The World."
> – Mahatma Ghandi

One of the best investments you can make in your integrity and your success is to take 100% responsibility for your life, your actions, your decisions and your results. The truth is there is only one person who is responsible for your life and that's you. Taking responsibility though, means giving up blaming others and outside circumstances. It eliminates excuses and victim stories. It means owning your mistakes, apologizing and making amends. In short, taking responsibility is what separates the few from the crowd.

Responsibility can be broken up into two words: Response – Ability. The ability to respond is what we really control. One of my favorite teachings of The Chicken Soup For The Soul creator, Jack Canfield is his formula:

$$E + R = O$$
(Event + Response = Outcome)

You and I can't control the event: the economy, our boss, our spouse, the weather, racism, someone's attitude, gender bias, the government, lack of support, etc.

The events are the way things are. We can't change the way things are, we can only change the way we are. Whether we respond or react. That response ultimately creates the outcome, the O.

Most people tend to blame and focus on the event, the E. Why me? It isn't fair? Why did that have to happen? If it only would have been different.

Ultimately, if you are going to take 100% responsibility for your life, you need to let go of the E and focus instead on what you do control, the R. When we focus on the R, we begin to change our thinking, our communication, our behavior, and our results.

Begin today taking total responsibility for your life by focusing on the R of the E + R = O formula. When you begin to change your responses, your life will begin to get better as a result.

3) Keep Promises and Fulfill Commitments

> Breach of promise is a base surrender of truth.
> – Mahatma Gandhi

Stephen Covey explained, "The power to make and keep commitments to ourselves is the basic habit of effectiveness." People who keep promises and fulfill commitments are not only recognized for their effectiveness, but also their integrity.

A wonderful example of the power of keeping commitments comes from my good friend and Olympic Gold Medalist, Peter Vidmar, who relates this story.

"It was the summer of 1979 and things were going very well in my training. I was at the U.S. Olympic Festival, which was held that year on the campus of the United States Air Force Academy in Colorado Springs. I was on my way to a fifth-place-finish that would pave the way for my qualifying for my first world championship team. Every morning before that day's competition I would meet Mako (Peter's Coach, Mako Sakamoto) in the middle of the quad at the center of the campus. It's a huge quad, surrounded by the campus and the Rocky Mountains beyond – a very inspiring setting all by itself.

Mako and I would run around the quad in that thin mountain air, always finishing with a short, fast sprint. (I enjoyed racing Mako – sprinting was the one thing I could beat him at. I could blow him away.) After running we'd do some stretches and some exercises and go over our routine for the day. Then we'd have breakfast.

About midway through the week Mako looked at me and said, "Pete, do you know what a vow is?"

Whenever Mako asked questions I'd get nervous. I knew he always had a motive behind them, and that motive usually involved more work for me.

"A what?" I said. I guess I was buying time.
"A vow," he said.
"Yeah," I answered. "I know what a vow is."

"Lets make a vow," he said. "Let's vow that you will do morning training before breakfast like this until you graduate from college and I will too."

So what was I going to say? No?

"Uh, OK," I said.

"Let's shake on it."

So we shook on it and when we did, when I shook his hand, even though there was no drum roll, no trumpets blaring and no lawyers were writing it down, I knew it was binding. I thought, "I have to do this." Which was great at the time. I was 18 years old. I was having the best meet of my life. I was fired up.

But I hadn't even started college yet.

Keeping that vow was a piece of cake for the first couple of months, when I was healthy, when I didn't have any early classes. And even after I started my freshman year at UCLA that fall, and I did have early classes, it wasn't that tough at first. But I knew it wouldn't always be easy to keep that vow, and I was right. It's not easy when you've blown your ankle out the day before at practice, so you can't even run, you can't even walk, and even to try that is stupid because you should be resting the ankle. It's not easy when you're tired and sore and you're behind in your homework.

I can remember being sick with the flu and doing the morning run barely moving. I can remember doing it in pouring rain. I did it when I had a fever and the very worst thing I could have done was get out of bed, and yet I got out of bed, more than once and did that workout. Every morning. Six days every week. (Sundays off) Warm-up, stretch, do something productive. That was the deal. If I slept in, I'd miss class if I had to, but I'd get that workout in. Even when I was on an airplane I'd work out before breakfast. That was probably tougher than being sick. I remember being on an overseas airplane going to an international meet, and waking up and looking at Mako doing pushups in the aisle. People were looking at him like he was nuts. I'd think, "This is so embarrassing," but I'd get down and do my pushups.

I never missed a day. I'd made a commitment and I was going to stick with it, NO MATTER WHAT. I had to.

It didn't make sense at times. Sometimes it was physiologically the wrong thing to do too. Sometimes I'd just be making myself worse. But that only applied to the physical side of things. Keeping that vow made me so much tougher in my mind. Psychologically it was always the right thing to do. It made me think I could handle anything."

4) Build People Up, Don't Tear People Down

> "I look only to the good qualities of men. Not being faultless myself, I won't presume to probe into the faults of others."
> – Mahatma Gandhi

People with integrity focus their attention on building up others as opposed to tearing them down. They avoid criticism, complaining and gossip and instead they celebrate the successes and praise the strengths of those around them. It is easy to get caught in the trap of gossip or negative speaking, but I love what Will Durrant said when he stated, "to speak ill of others is a dishonest way of praising ourselves."

Do you build people up or tear people down?

To illustrate this point further, let me tell you about an interesting study. Friends Gary Hamel and C.K. Prahalad wrote about a study conducted with a group of monkeys.

Four monkeys were placed in a room that had a tall pole in the center. Suspended from the top of that pole was a bunch of bananas. One of the hungry monkeys started climbing the pole to get something to eat, but just as he reached out to grab a banana, he was doused with a bucket of cold water. Squealing, he scampered down the pole and abandoned his attempt to feed himself. Each monkey made a similar attempt, and each one was drenched with cold water. After making several attempts, they finally gave up.

Then the researchers removed one of the monkeys from the room and replaced him with a new monkey. As the newcomer began to climb the pole, the other three grabbed him and pulled him down to the ground. After trying to climb the pole several times and being dragged down by the others, he finally gave up and never attempted to climb again.

The researchers replaced the original monkeys one by one, and each time a new monkey was brought in he would be dragged down by the others before he could reach the bananas. In time, the room was filled with monkeys who had never received a cold shower. However, none of them would climb the pole, and not one of them knew why.

What kind of person (monkey) are you? Do you build people up or tear people down?

5) Give 100%, 100% of The Time

> "Satisfaction lies in the effort, not in the attainment, full effort is full victory."
> – Mahatma Gandhi

Do you give 100% at work, at school, and at home? Some people probably think of giving 100% this way: 12% for Monday, 23% for Tuesday, 40% for Wednesday, 20% for Thursday, 5% for Friday = 100%

Too many people coast through life, only doing what is required to get by. Giving 100%, 100% of the time is the effort required to stop getting by and start getting ahead. It is the difference between playing not to lose and playing to win. Living by design and not default. Giving 100% will separate you from the rest. It will build your integrity and your results.

John Wooden was one of the greatest basketball coaches of all time. His ten NCAA national championships in a 12-year period while at UCLA are unmatched by any other college basketball coach. John used to tell his players, "Give 100% today, because you can't make up for it by giving 110% tomorrow. You don't have 110%, you only have 100%, and that's what I want from you right now."

Giving 100%, 100% of the time builds a reputation of dependability. It allows you to build your character and your capacity. It is an investment in integrity that will transform your results. Patricia Aburdene, author of "Megatrends 2010" said, "Transcendent values like trust and integrity, literally translate into revenue, profits and prosperity."

Give 100%, 100% of the time and you will gain respect and a reputation for getting things done.

6) Be Humble

"As human beings, our greatness lies not so much in being able to remake the world - that is the myth of the atomic age - as in being able to remake ourselves."
– Mahatma Gandhi

Humility is a key to integrity and influence. People with humility are always learning, growing and developing. They successfully keep their ego at bay while remaining confident in their capability. Humility doesn't mean being passive or weak. It is the attribute of being open and teachable.

Following World War II, W. Edwards Deming was sent to Japan by the U.S. Government to help the war-torn country in its efforts to revive its economic base. While in Japan, his expertise in quality control techniques attracted the attention of Japanese business leaders and engineers. Eventually, Deming trained hundreds of engineers, managers, and scholars in statistical process control and concepts of quality. Deming's message to Japan's chief executives was that improving quality would reduce expenses while increasing productivity and market share.

Deming's teaching focused on the Japanese word, "kaizen." Translated it means, "constant change for the better." Through this philosophy the Japanese economy was revitalized because of consistent effort to learn, do and become better.

Humility is the foundation of kaizen. Improvement begins when we become compliant students, ready and willing to explore ways we can become better, contribute more, and live according to principle.

Stephen M.R. Covey said, "So how does humility manifest itself in leadership and in life? A humble person is more concerned about *what* is right than about *being right*, about *acting* on good ideas than *having* good ideas, about *embracing* new truth than *defending* outdated position, about *building* the team than *exalting self*, about *recognizing contribution* than being *recognized* for making it."

Developing humility is an essential investment in integrity. It makes leaders approachable, because they are open and willing to adapt. It makes businessmen and women trustworthy because they live according to principle. It takes the ego, arrogance and selfishness out of relationships, allowing people to connect and their associations to flourish.

7) Live Your Values

"Happiness is when what you think, what you say, and what you do are in harmony."
– Mahatma Gandhi

Values are the principles by which we live our lives. Principles such as: honesty, cleanliness, respect, hard work, love, freedom, progress, service. Values are subjective and vary across people and cultures. What one person esteems important another might deem unimportant. When you know what you value you can begin to live according to your conscience. Integrity is when you live what you profess. It is being whole, not saying one thing and doing another. It is important to understand what we value but even more important to live in line with the values we profess. Brian Tracy explained the result of living our values when he said, "You are the very happiest when what you're doing on the outside is congruent with your values on the inside. When you are living in alignment with what you feel to be right, good, and true, you'll automatically feel positive and confident about yourself and your world"

A great example of this surfaced recently on an international stage at the Olympic Games in Beijing, China. In the semifinals tennis match for men's singles, American James Blake was facing Fernando Gonzalez of Chile. The match lasted nearly three hours before Gonzalez won and advanced to the gold medal match. But that was not the story.

On the first point of the third to last game, Gonzalez served the ball and then approached the net. Blake tried to pass Gonzalez by hitting a shot right at him and the ball went long. When the point was awarded to Gonzalez, Blake approached the umpire to argue that the ball had nicked Gonzalez' racquet as it passed and therefore should be his point. The chair umpire said he didn't see it and according to the rules they could not use replay to review the shot. (Such was not the case for those watching on television around the world; the tv replay clearly showed that the ball hit Gonzalez' racquet).

Frustrated with the situation Blake turned and looked directly at Gonzalez. After a long pause, getting no response from his opponent, he returned to the baseline and they continued the game. In the press conference afterward Blake revealed a lot about his own values: "Playing in the Olympics, in what's supposed to be considered a gentleman's sport, that's a time to call it on yourself. Fernando looked me square in the eye and didn't call it."

"I'm 100% sure it hit his racquet," Blake told reporters. "If the roles were reversed, my father would have pulled me off the court. We know when the ball touches us. And he knew. You call it yourself because it is the right thing to do."

The Olympics provided a perfect backdrop for this lesson on values. Blake vented, "Maybe I shouldn't expect people to hold themselves to a high standard of sportsmanship, but yes, maybe I did expect a little more out of the Olympics."

James Blake called out his opponent, something few athletes do. For him though, it was the right thing to do because of the values he believes and lives by. Thomas Jefferson eloquently stated, "In matters of style, swim with the current; in matters of principle stand like a rock."

ROI

Any investor knows that the success of an investment depends on the ROI, the Return On Investment. ROI is a performance measure used to judge the efficiency of an investment. What do you get in return?

When you invest in integrity, your ROI comes by way of increased trust, credibility and reputation, three of the major tenets of lasting influence.

Trust is simply confidence in character. It's the underlying foundation for healthy leadership, as well as business and personal relationships. Art Jonak said, "When someone trusts both your knowledge and your motives, they are open to your influence."

> "If my people understand me, I'll get their attention. If my people trust me, I'll get their action."
> – Cavett Robert

Credibility is a confidence in both character and capability. When you are credible in people's eyes you carry clout. They are willing to listen to your ideas and opinion and are open to your influence. If you are humble: always learning and growing, keep commitments, and give 100% - 100% of the time, then your capability and results will grow along with your character. You will quickly become credible, a person of influence, an opinion leader. In the book, Influencer the authors point out the characteristics of Opinion Leader. "People, including children, pay attention to individuals who possess two important qualities. First, these people are viewed as knowledgeable about the issue at hand. They tend to stay connected to their area of expertise, often through a variety of sources. Second, opinion leaders are viewed as trustworthy. They don't merely know a great deal about a certain area, but they also have other people's best interest in mind. This means that they aren't seen as using their knowledge to manipulate or harm, but rather to help. If others believe that you're missing either of these two qualities, you won't be very influential."

> "To be persuasive we must be believable; to be believable we must be credible; to be credible we must be truthful."
> – Edward Morrow

There's a fundamental rule of business that states: "People do business with people they know, like and trust." We've all heard that, and even repeated it, but ultimately it is wrong. Ok, maybe wrong is not the right word. But the rule is incomplete. The truth is, people do business with people they know, like, trust and VALUE.

Honesty and likeability are important, but if people don't see you as valuable, they will never do business with you. If you don't come across as professional, knowledgeable, and credible with the right skill set to get the job done, you will never be as influential and successful as you would like.

So what do we do about it? How do we make ourselves more valuable? By constantly developing our knowledge, our skills and continually striving to get better.

The fundamental rule of Business should read: "People do business with people they know, like, trust and value"

Reputation is your track record. It is confidence in character and capability over time. Henry Ford said, "You can't build a reputation on what you are going to do," so reputation only comes after you make the investment. Lasting influence is built and sustained by reputation. People can be influential in a given situation, or for a temporary period of time, but lasting influence is based in reputation. That is why it is so important to guard your reputation, cultivate your reputation, and be a person of character and ever-increasing capability.

> "Reputation is built by one thousand individual acts and lost by just one" – Unknown

FIVE APPLICATIONS OF INFLUENCE

When it comes to real, genuine, lasting influence, people follow because of who you are (integrity) and how you treat them (interaction). Bob Burg and John David Mann put it in perfect prose: "Your influence is determined by how abundantly you place other people's interests first."

So how do you place other people's interests first? How do you not only have people buy into you but also buy into your actions? How do you interact with people in a way that makes them feel that you have their best interest in mind and therefore causes them to trust you, listen to you, follow you, do business with you and ultimately be influenced by you?

There are five applications of influence. Five specific, applicable practices that will make your interactions not only enjoyable, but effectively influential. Five ways that you can place other people's interests first.
The Five Applications of Influence are:

The Five Applications of Influence are:
1) Develop Outward Thinking
2) Invest In People
3) Focus on Being Interested, Not Interesting
4) Practice The Platinum Rule
5) Seek To Serve

In the next five chapters we will address each of these one by one. With example, instruction and real world application, you will begin to grow your influence in leadership, in business and relationships. You will become a person of influence.

DEVELOP OUTWARD THINKING

Chapter 3

DEVELOP OUTWARD THINKING

"Self-discipline begins with the mastery of your thoughts. If you don't control what you think, you can't control what you do. Simply, self-discipline enables you to think first and act afterward."
– Napoleon Hill

The most effective formula for exerting real, positive and lasting influence on others is to consistently think of others first.

Gordon B. Hinckley, a personal hero of mine, once said, "The best antidote for worry is work. The best medicine for despair is service. The best cure for weariness is to help someone even more tired."

He recalled a time early in his life when he was far from home on an assignment, feeling forlorn, abandoned and discouraged, and he received a simple piece of unexpected advice that transformed his life:

"I wrote a letter home to my good father and said that I felt I was wasting my time and his money. My father was a wise and inspired man. He wrote a very short letter to me, which said, 'Dear Gordon, I have your recent letter. I have only one suggestion: forget yourself and go to work.'"

Placing other people's interests first starts with our thinking. It begins as a mindset, an attitude, and it's that other-oriented thinking that drives behavior that is both uncommon and powerful.

FIVE APPLICATIONS OF INFLUENCE

It's not about you - it's about them! The focus of an influencer is always on the audience.

If you are a speaker – it's about the people listening to you.
If you are in sales – it's about your customer or prospect.
If you are a leader – it's about the people you are leading.
If you are a teacher – it's about your students.
If you are a parent – it's about your children

Almost everyone has this backwards. They think being influential means they need to become polished or powerful. Influence, though, is all about the audience. Be it an audience of one or one thousand. When it's about them, they get it, and we grow in their eyes.

By thinking out instead of in, by concentrating on others instead of on us, a tremendous transformation takes place. We go from inner directed to outer directed, from taker to giver, from self-centered to others-focused, from tightfisted to generous, from shortsighted to farsighted, from selfish to selfless. We begin to see and act on behalf of others' needs ahead of our own; our thoughts are in terms of "we" instead of "me."

"There is no *I* in *TEAM*. But there is an *M* and an *E* and that spells *ME!*"

Amazing things happen when our first priority is concern for others. We forget ourselves. Personal worries and concerns that once felt confining all but disappear. Among the most legendary stories in wartime are tales of the heroic performance of medics, who have received medals for valor far out of proportion to their numbers. The reason can be found in their assignment: to care for the wounded, wherever they might fall. To carry out their duty they forget all else and concentrate solely on taking care of others. Their own interests and needs become secondary, and they accomplish great things.

Numerous studies have shown that people who are selfish tend toward worry, loneliness, anger and unhappiness. People who eliminate "I" and focus on others are much happier -- and exert much greater influence --in the long run. A study conducted by professors at the University of British Columbia and the Harvard Business School showed that when people received unexpected financial bonuses at work, those who spent the money on others reported greater happiness, even though they had less money. "It's possible to buy happiness after all," the researchers concluded – "When you spend money on others."

Throughout history, this outward-thinking key to happiness, success and far-reaching influence has been realized and implemented by leaders in all walks of life. It's been given many names: pay-it-forward ... circle of giving ... pass it on ... chain of love. Time after time, its worth has been proven, its virtues extolled by those who recognize its value and reap its benefits. But despite its unparalleled record of success and ease of implementation (anyone can do it), the simple practice of outward thinking remains largely unemployed – a mindset openly available, and enormously beneficial, but often ignored.

> "All that a man achieves, all that he fails to achieve, is the direct result of his own thoughts."
> – James Allen

ELEPHANT MINDSET

When I was 19 years old I had a mentor who taught me a lot about the importance of correct thinking. He told me that anything was possible if we had the right thinking. What Henry Ford said is true: "Whether you think you can or you think you can't, you're right!"

One way my mentor helped me to understand the power of your thoughts was through the example of elephants. He said, "When a baby elephant is born in captivity, the captors will use a large, heavy chain to tie the elephant's leg to a solid post, driven deep into the ground. The baby elephant will pull and pull with all its might, but will not be able to break the grip of the chain. After enough pulling, the elephant learns that it can't escape and begins to think, "What is the use in trying. I'll never break free." As the elephant grows in size and strength, it develops enough strength to break free, but the captors can replace the chain with a simple string that will keep the elephant tied to the stake. The grown elephant is not limited at all by his captors, but by his thinking.

INWARD THINKING IS TOTALLY UNATTRACTIVE

"Selfishness is the greatest curse of the human race."
– William E. Gladstone

We were 17, we had dated for a couple of months (which may have been a record) and one day we were at my house and she said, "You know what your problem is?" – I know, that's never a good start to a conversation – but I bit my tongue and against my better judgment I asked, "What?" And she said, "You always have to one-up people."

I said, "What do you mean?" and she said, "You're never genuinely excited for other people, you just want to tell them why you're so great."

I fought back and said, "That's not true," and then she gave me an example: "Let's say you meet someone and you ask them what they like to do and they say they like to play basketball. Instead of being excited that they play basketball, you react by saying, 'I play basketball too. I'm the starting point guard on the basketball team. Our team is undefeated this year and I'm leading the team in assists.'"

She hit me square between the eyes. I was speechless, because she was right. Then she said something you never want to hear from your girlfriend: "Your selfish thinking is totally unattractive."

It's not easy being selfless. It's not easy thinking of others and putting them first. Being outwardly focused requires self-discipline, dedication and repetition. Paying attention to others, adding value to their lives, celebrating their triumphs, influencing them in a positive way – it doesn't become a habit until you do it over and over again. That elusive and magnetic characteristic we call charisma doesn't just happen.

CHARISMA

> "Charisma is a sparkle in people that money can't buy.
> It's an invisible energy with visible effects."
> – Marianne Williamson

I met Kenton Worthington seven years ago. He's one of the most successful young entrepreneurs I know. I remember coming home the day we were introduced and telling my wife I'd just met one of the most charismatic people I'd ever known. She said what does that mean? And I sat there trying to figure out what charismatic meant. Why would I describe him as charismatic?

My first response was it's his personality. I said, 'You know what I mean, he's got a charismatic personality.' And she said, 'No, I don't know what that means. What makes his personality charismatic?' Still stumped for an intelligent answer, after that, I began to closely watch Kenton in business and personal settings; I paid close attention to how he interacted with people, how he talked, what he said, how he listened, his body language, all in an effort to try to define what charisma is all about.

The first thing I noticed is that he's optimistic, he's always got a smile on his face, he's constantly up, he's positive, he's uplifting, he's enthusiastic about the past, the present and the future.

But I sensed there was more to charisma than being optimistic. I then noticed that Kenton has a lot of energy to go along with that optimism. He's active; he's full of life. When he talks to people he's engaged. There's a lot of expression and emotion in his face and in his body language.

But I sensed there was more to charisma than being optimistic. I then noticed Kenton has a lot of energy to go along with that optimism. He's active; he's full of life. When he talks to people he's engaged. There's a lot of expression and emotion in his face and in his body language.

But that can't be all of it either, I thought. I've met other people with a lot of energy -- and other people with a lot of optimism -- that I wouldn't describe as charismatic.

I then determined that it must be because he's confident. He has a can-do attitude, a take-over-the-game kind of style. I think confidence has a lot to do with charisma. You can't be charismatic without it. So confidence is an important ingredient too, but it's just that. It's an ingredient.

Finally, after watching Kenton for several years I came to the conclusion that optimism, energy and confidence play a role in his charisma. But beyond all those fine qualities, he is genuinely focused on other people. That, I decided, is what sets him apart. It's what gives him that elusive quality of charisma. When you have a conversation with Kenton it's about you, not about him. He asks questions, he shows real excitement over your successes and concern over your challenges. He finds ways to genuinely compliment whoever he's talking to and engages in a way that makes the other person feel better about themselves. So to answer my wife's question, "What is Charisma?" It's a mix of ingredients – optimism, energy, confidence – but more than anything else it's based on outward rather than inward thinking. That's Kenton's secret -- and, I'm convinced, the secret of other charismatic influencers -- and it's really no secret at all.

It was civil rights activist Cornel West who said, "Humility means two things. One, a capacity for self-criticism … The second feature is allowing others to shine, affirming others, empowering and enabling others. Those who lack humility are dogmatic and egotistical. That masks a deep sense of insecurity. They feel the success of others is at the expense of their own fame and glory."

"If you would win a man to your cause, said Abraham Lincoln, "first convince him that you are his sincere friend."

"Some singers want the audience to love them. I love the audience," said the wildly popular tenor Luciano Pavarotti.

LITMUS TEST

Below are 12 questions you can ask yourself. They will help you to see whether your thinking is inward or outward, selfish or selfless. They are not designed to make you feel bad. Rather, they should help you stop and really analyze your thinking and your motives. Be honest with yourself. We can all improve our thinking. These questions will help you accurately assess where you are and in what areas you can improve.

1. In sales do you A) care more about the commission you make or B) more about the customer?

2. In leadership do you A) place blame or B) praise your people?

3. Do you A) feel threatened by the success of others or B) celebrate their triumphs?

4. In relationships do you A) try and change others or B) try to make yourself better?

5. In relationships do you A) want to win or B) do you want win-win?

6. When accidents happen do you A) respond with anger and annoyance or B) with care and concern?

7. When you're part of a team, do you A) concentrate on what you can do to excel individually or B) on what you can do to help the team excel?

8. If you're slicing a cake, do you A) give the largest piece to yourself or B) to your companion?

9. In defeat do you A) make excuses and alibis or B) give credit to your opponent?

10. In social settings do you befriend the loners and make people feel comfortable?

11. Do you give more compliments than you receive?

12. Do you keep score?

If your answers to Numbers 1 through 9 are all B and your answers to 10 through 12 are "Yes" you get an A on the outward thinking test.

A LESSON FROM A CHILD

My two-year-old, Tanner, loves his older sister Andie, who is four. He follows her around, copies her every action, wants what she wants, explores where she explores. I've noticed that every time I give Tanner a piece of gum, a cookie, fruit snacks, a drink, or a prize, he invariably asks for one for Andie. He does this instinctively, without hesitation and without thinking. Sometimes she's not even there, but he'll still ask for it, and then he will save it for her. It is an unspoken demonstration of outward thinking, of looking out for another. It's the way we all should be.

INVEST IN PEOPLE

Chapter 4

INVEST IN PEOPLE

> The best minute you spend is the one you invest in people.
> – Ken Blanchard

My favorite sport in high school was basketball. At age sixteen I still believed I would be an NBA star. In the fall of my junior year I decided to run cross-country to get in better shape for basketball season. I wanted to be in the best condition of my life. Cross-country was going well, I enjoyed the team, the practices and the competition. Then, about a mile into the first meet, I stepped in a hole as I rounded a corner and I heard my knee pop. To make a long story short, my cross-county career was over but basketball was also out for the season.

I suddenly had extra time on my hands. To help fill it, a good friend encouraged me to get involved in a school club called DECA. I learned that DECA is a leadership and business organization for high school and college

students, which trains future leaders in entrepreneurship, sales, management and marketing. DECA is a great
program. As part of the program students from around
the country compete in business competitions, first at the
district level, then at state and finally at nationals.

I chose to compete in the Entrepreneurship category
which meant that I conceived of a business, developed a
business plan and presented it to judges who were acting
as venture capitalists. The judge's grades were based on
how convinced they were to invest in the business.

I won the district competition, which meant I qualified
for the Colorado State finals in Colorado Springs. I was
ecstatic and even more so when I took first at state. I had
qualified for nationals, which were held that year in Louisville, Kentucky.

Overall there were about 10,000 kids who competed in the
entrepreneurship category. Nationals, however, was just
the top 100, or two from every state. The first round took
the 100 contestants and narrowed it down to 50. My presentation in the first round went well and I made the cut for
the top 50. The second round brought another set of pre-
sentations and then they narrowed it down to the top 15. I

was sweating bullets as I was the 15th name called for the top 15, but I made it. In the last round, there was one final presentation in front of the judges and then they brought the top 15 on stage and announced 5th place, 4th place, 3rd place, 2nd place and finally the the 1st place winner.

I'd given this presentation thousands of times. I gave it to my parents. I gave it to my teachers. I gave it to my classmates. I gave it in the mirror. I gave it at districts. I gave it at state. And I gave it in the first couple of rounds at nationals. But I had never given a presentation like the final round of nationals. It went perfect. The judges were engaged, they laughed at my jokes, they asked questions about my business plan, I hit all my points and I felt like it was the best presentation I had ever given. I left that presentation knowing that I had done my very best and I thought I had won nationals. Well, I didn't win nationals. I ended up taking second (and I'm sure the girl in first place cheated but I can't prove it). But I learned a tremendous lesson at nationals.

After my presentation the head judge, a prominent businessman in Louisville, gave me his card and said, "Please call me, I would love to help you get going in business." I was 17 years old and I kind of laughed and said, "Thanks, but this is just a competition. I am not really trying to start this business."

Then he said something that has stuck with me ever since. He said, "I always get my highest return on investment when I invest in people, and I want to invest in you." Wow – what a lesson! Think about that one for a minute.

I've come to realize that he wasn't interested in investing in my business ideas, he was interested in investing in me. Investing in people is paramount to building relationships, genuine connection and lasting influence. So the question is, who are you investing in? In business, in leadership, in personal relationships, are you investing in people?

When I say invest, my mind automatically thinks money, but investing in people is not about money. When you invest in people you invest time, energy, emotion, care, understanding, love, patience, interest, thought, friendship and concern.

> "If you want 1 year of happiness – grow grain
> If you want 10 years of happiness – grow trees
> If you want 100 years of happiness – grow people"
> -Chinese Proverb

CARE: A GREAT INVESTMENT

As a leader it is imperative that you invest in your people everyday. You've heard about going the extra mile, reaching above and beyond. If you want to be a person of influence, going the extra mile is exactly what investing in people is all about.

Let me give you a great example of that.

In 2003 on "Good Morning America," Charlie Gibson was interviewing General Earl Hailston of the United States Marine Corps. General Hailson and his Marines were stationed a few miles outside of Iraq waiting to go to war.

Throughout the interview they discussed the morale of the troops, and the plan and purpose of the mission. Then at the end of the interview, Charlie asked an interesting question. He said, "General do you have any hobbies, anything that you like to do other than your career?" General Hailston replied, "I do, I love photography and particularly taking pictures of my men." He continued, "I like to go out during the day and I take pictures of my men and then at night I email them with a short note to their moms back home."

Intrigued, Charlie responded, "Really, would you mind sharing what you say?" General Hailston said, "no problem." Then he opened the computer and read the last email he had sent.

This is what it said,

Dear Mrs. Johnson,
I thought you might enjoy seeing this picture of your son. He is doing great. I also wanted you to know that you did a wonderful job of raising him. You must be very proud. I can certainly tell you that I'm honored to serve with him in the U.S. Marines.

General Earl Hailston

Did you get goose bumps when you read that? I don't believe that any where in the job description of a Marine General it says, "Make sure to send emails to worried mothers." General Hailston, though, is an above and beyond leader, who knows the importance of investing in his people. Investing in people is outward thinking put into practical application. In the grand scheme of things, an email is a very small thing, but I'm sure it wasn't if you ask Mrs. Johnson.

"People don't care how much you know until they know how much you care."
-Cavett Robert

INVESTMENTS LEAD TO STORIES

Investments in people lead to stories. And the stories that are told invariably build the influence and reputation of the one doing the investing. Think about it:

· When you have exceptional service at a restaurant, what do you do? You tell the story.
· When your boss does something extra special for you, what do you do? You tell the story.
· When a friend goes out of their way to help you, what do you do? You tell the story.

We love it when someone invests in us by providing exceptional attention and service, and because it is so unexpected or unusual, we almost always share.

One of my clients is Subway. I speak to their franchisees and managers quite often and when I do I always share a simple experience to illustrate this point. I was eating in a subway once in the middle of the afternoon and the store was empty. The teenager who was working behind the counter at one point came over to my table and asked, "Would you like me to get you a refill?" It was a simple gesture but one that stuck out to me because he didn't need to do it and it took a little extra effort.

I tell the franchisees and managers my story because I want them to recognize that their customers tell stories too, and when they learn to invest in their customers by going above and beyond, those stories will help to bring them more business. It's really true that the best form of advertising is a happy customer telling your story.

LITTLE THINGS MATTER

Todd Smith has had tremendous success. Interestingly enough, though, he doesn't have a fancy formula or complicated concept of how to succeed. He, instead, simply attributes it to the little things that matter most.

At the age of 23, Todd began a career as a residential real estate agent. He became a student of personal development and within four and half years was one of the nation's top-selling Realtors, selling over 115 homes a year. At 28, he was one of the youngest Realtors ever inducted into RE/MAX's Hall of Fame.

From real estate, he expanded into direct sales, and for the past 20 years Todd Smith has owned his own sales and marketing business in the direct selling industry. His business has generated more than one billion dollars in sales and has paid him more than 23 million dollars in commissions.

Todd has become an internationally recognized leader in the direct selling industry and the personal development field. He has conducted more than 1,000 training sessions and seminars for audiences around the world and has also developed numerous training manuals and audio-visual sales tools, teaching entrepreneurs how to achieve professional success and accomplish their personal goals.

Todd believes that it's the little things that matter most; that make the biggest difference. And he is now sharing that message with the world. Over 200,000 of Todd's blog posts at www.littlethingsmatter.com are being read every month and his podcasts are ranked #38 in America"s Top 100 Podcasts. Todd's forthcoming book is titled, (you guessed it) "Little Things Matter."

> "Enjoy the little things, for one day you may look back
> and realize they were the big things."
> – Robert Brault

Little things do matter and when it comes to investing in
people it's often the little things that make the biggest difference. Below are 30 little investments that you can use
to make a positive impact in someone's life. These investments are small and simple gestures. But when implemented in leadership, in business and in relationships,
they have tremendous power.

30 POWERFUL INVESTMENTS IN PEOPLE

1) Smile
2) Write a thank-you note
3) Remember someone's name
4) Wish someone Happy Birthday
5) Really listen
6) Open a door
7) Support their activities
8) Call just to say hello
9) Buy them their favorite treat
10) Point out something they've done well
11) Encourage

12) Give a Gift
13) Reach out just because
14) Remember personal facts
15) Be courteous
16) Celebrate their victories with them (big or small)
17) Go out of your way to promote their agenda
18) Notice a new hair style/cut
19) Apologize
20) Give a book or article they would be interested in
21) Mow your neighbor's lawn
22) Share a joke or funny moment/experience
23) Say thank you
24) Give flowers or something to brighten their day
25) Give a hug
26) Compliment sincerely
27) Bite your tongue (refrain from criticism/complaint)
28) Pay for lunch
29) Include those usually excluded
30) Praise Publicly

IT ADDS UP

Many of the investments listed above may seem trivial. They aren't. In working with people they are crucial. They are the difference-makers. And as these "little things" add up they collectively create enormous influence.

On the slopes of Long's Peak in Colorado lay the ruins of a gigantic tree. Naturalists tell us that it stood for some 400 years. It was a seedling when Columbus landed at San Salvador, and half grown when the Pilgrims settled at Plymouth. During the course of its long life, it was struck by lightning 14 times and the innumerable avalanches and storms of four centuries thundered past it. It survived them all. In the end, however, an army of beetles attacked the tree and leveled it to the ground. The insects ate their way throughout the bark and gradually destroyed the inner strength of the tree by their tiny, but incessant attacks. A forest giant which age had not withered, nor lightning blasted, nor storms subdued, fell at last before beetles so small that a man could crush them between his forefinger and his thumb.

Just as small combined efforts of beetles can destroy, so likewise can small investments of love, care and kindness have a building effect in our relationships and a major impact on the people we influence.

It's the little things that make the biggest difference.

FOCUS ON BEING INTERESTED, NOT INTERESTING

Chapter 5

FOCUS ON BEING INTERESTED, NOT INTERESTING

"You can make more friends in two months by becoming interested in other people than you can in two years by trying to get other people interested in you."
- Dale Carnegie

A couple of years ago a friend called me and asked if we could talk. She came over to my house and began explaining to me how unhappy she was. She was in her first year of college and was feeling like she wasn't making friends, dating much or enjoying college life. As I listened, she kept saying she wished she were more interesting, and that people wanted to get to know her better. (I'm sure we have all felt like that at some time in our lives). After I listened to her story, I asked if I could make a suggestion that would help her connect to others, be well liked, and attract and influence people. "Of course," she said. Then I said: "focus on being interested, not interesting."

The problem with being interesting is it's all about you. But being interested is all about the other person. It's where influence comes from. It's placing other people's interests first.

> "I went out to find a friend, but could not find one there. I went out to be a friend and friends were everywhere"
> – James Merritt

Have you ever had a conversation with someone where you did almost all the talking? Most of us probably come away from that conversation thinking, "That was a great conversation!" It's true; people love to talk. We love to share our thoughts, our ideas, our opinions. We love to tell interesting stories and make people laugh. We all have a little bit of that in us.

People who are interested, though, know how valuable it is for relationships and friendships to let the other person talk. They listen more than they talk. They allow others to share ideas and opinions. They make people feel welcome, involved and appreciated.

So how do we do it?

BE PRESENT

One of the simplest ways to show genuine interest is to be present in conversations. When we focus on the person we are talking to, we show them that we care. If we are distracted, multitasking, or our thought process is somewhere else; it makes others feel that they are unimportant to us.

When someone is not present in the conversation, it can be annoying at best and sometimes even hurtful. And yet, we are probably all guilty of this at different times. Below is a list of some of the major offenses:

- Texting while someone is talking
- Emailing while talking on the phone
- Watching TV while someone is talking (in person or on the phone)
- Looking around the room when someone is talking

When we are fully present in conversations it is validating to the person we are talking to. It tells them that they are important and that we care.

ASKING QUESTIONS

> "Successful people ask better questions, and as a result, they get better answers."
> – Anthony Robbins

Being interested starts by asking questions.

As we strive to build our influence and rapport with people, we all need to know more of what other people are feeling and thinking, wanting and planning. To do this, we need to use questions that "open" people up instead of "closing" them off. Our usual "yes/no" questions actually tend to shut people up rather than opening them up.

You can encourage others to share more of their thoughts and feelings by asking the right questions. Open-ended questions allow for a wide range of responses. For example, asking "What did you like best about that movie/speech/food, etc.?" will evoke a more in-depth response than "Did you like it?" (Which could be answered with a simple "yes" or "no"). If you do ask yes/no questions, be ready to follow them up with probing questions that will move the response beyond a one-word answer. "Are you having a good day?" – "Yes." "What has made it so good?"

Asking questions is like any other skill. It can be learned, understood and mastered with study, practice and persistence.

The idea behind asking questions is to show interest, learn more, and make the other person feel good. To do this, start with feel good areas that establish rapport. FORM is an acronym standing for Family, Occupation, Recreation and Money - basic building blocks of life that people are interested in talking about. Here are some examples of FORM questions:

- "What have you been doing with your free time?"
- "How is the economy treating you?"
- "What projects have you been working on?"
- "I'd love to know more about your family. What are your kids involved in?"

As we learn to ask good questions. I'll share three of my favorite questions to ask. I've found that they invariably produce meaningful conversation. I like to call them the story question, the passion question, and Larry King's favorite question.

The Story Question: "How did you get started in the (XYZ) business?

Everyone loves to tell his or her story. So ask a question that allows them to do it. "How did you get started in (whatever it is they do)?"

The Passion Question: "What do you love best about what you do?"

People love to talk about the things they are passionate about. So ask them for details and just watch the room light up. An example might be, "So you are a stay at home mom, that's great. What do you love best about being a mother?" Let people share their passion and excitement for what they do.

These two questions open people up because they have a chance to talk about two of the most important parts of their life.

The third question is designed to go deeper.

Larry King's Favorite Question: "Why?"

Larry King makes a living as a talk show host; asking questions is what he does. He interviews everyone from top celebrities to world leaders on "Larry King Live." He has often said his favorite question is "Why?" "Why did you do that?" "Why did you go there?" "Why did that interest you?" "Why is that important?"

That one, simple, three-letter word,– "Why?" – has enormous power. It probes. It digs. It illuminates. It gets to the heart of the matter. It puts thought process and motives into context. It is at the center of meaningful dialogue and understanding.

Remember, it's not the person talking who controls the conversation; it's the person asking the questions who controls the conversation.

LISTENING

> It seems rather incongruous that in a society of super sophisticated communication, we often suffer from a shortage of listeners
> – Erma Bombeck

In a study on face-to-face communication, UCLA psychology professor Albert Mehrabian discovered that there are three components that make up what is being communicated: words, tone of voice, and body language. And they all don't carry the same weight.

- What we say accounts for 7% of what is believed.
- The way we say it accounts for 38%.
- What others see accounts for 55%.

Those numbers may be surprising, but they uncover an important truth: when you are communicating there are many factors beyond your words that matter: Your eye contact, your posture, your tone of voice, your gestures, your facial expressions, all of that and more.

And on the other end of the conversation, when you are listening instead of talking, there are just as many factors beyond your hearing that matter. Do you make eye contact? Are you leaning toward the person, indicating concentration? Does your body language suggest that you are engaged and interested? Do your facial expressions show empathy and understanding?

Actively listening is about more than being silent. It is about validating the other person, making them feel important, cared for, and understood.

If our goal is to be interested, not interesting, then we need to shift from focusing on ourselves to focusing on others completely.

Most of us are guilty of either talking too much or when we are not talking, preparing what we are going to say next. We listen enough to prepare our rebuttal, reply or response. Instead of being interested, we try to be relatable. When you hear from a coworker, "I am so excited! I finally finished the project I have been working on for six months," do you reply, "I know what you mean, I just finished my project too." Or do you say, "That's awesome, tell me about it."

> There was an old owl lived in an oak,
> The more he heard, the less he spoke,
> The less he spoke, the more he heard,
> O, if men were all like that wise bird!
> – Punch Magazine

I thought I knew how to listen until I got married. Then I discovered that I knew how to listen passively, or listen to find a solution. I wasn't very adept at active listening -- the ability to listen to understand, not with the intent to reply. The way my friend Dave Blanchard says it is, "It is listening to understand their point of view without any judgment or need to fix them."

Have you ever had someone do that for you? Truly listen to the point that you feel validated? It's an amazing feeling. When someone shows true interest in you and empathetically listens, it is liberating and connecting.

AM I A GOOD LISTENER?

Steven Ash, "The Career Doctor" developed this listening test. It is a great way to see where you rate as a listener. Good luck!

Give yourself 4 points if the answer to the following questions is Always; three points for Usually; two points for Rarely; and one point for Never.

___ Do I allow the speaker to finish without interrupting?

___ Do I listen "between the lines"; that is for the subtext?

___ When writing a message, do I listen for and write down the key fact and phrases?

___ Do I repeat what the person just said to clarify the meaning?

___ Do I avoid getting hostile and/or agitated when I disagree with the speaker?

__ Do I tune out distractions when listening?

__ Do I make an effort to seem interested in what the other person is saying?

Scoring:

26 or higher – You are an excellent listener

22-25 – Better than average score

18 – 21 room for improvement

17 or lower – Get out there right away and start listening

> "Listening requires giving up our favorite human pastime, involvement in ourselves and our own self-interest."
> – Sonya Hamlin

GET PERSONAL

A while back I went to a networking event for lunch. There were about eighty people there and we were assigned to tables with eight at each table. Throughout lunch, the conversation was good, but it was somewhat awkward and very superficial. Everyone wore a nametag with their name and the name of their company, so the typical question was directed at the name of the company on the nametag. "Tell me about XYZ company?" or "What do you do at XYZ?"

Then the event director introduced an activity. We went around the table and each of us had two minutes to answer a personal question and then two minutes to talk about what we do professionally.

The personal question was either "What is a mistake you have made in the past?" or "What has been a memorable sporting event for you?"

I don't think it mattered what the personal questions were. What mattered is that they were personal. When people began to open up and talk about personal things, the mood, conversation and connection at the table changed. People were laughing and interacting more naturally. They were interested and engaged. The conversation was no longer superficial. It was genuine.

I came away from that experience with some clear realizations.

- When we can talk to people personally and not just professionally, we connect.

- When we open up personally, others can relate.
- When we are vulnerable and authentic, we allow others to be the same and we bond.

It's like the great quote from Marianne Williamson:

"Our deepest fear is not that we are inadequate. Our deepest fear is that we are powerful beyond measure. It is our light, not our darkness that most frightens us. We ask ourselves, who am I to be brilliant, gorgeous, talented, fabulous? Actually, who are you not to be? You are a child of God. Your playing small does not serve the world. There is nothing enlightened about shrinking so that other people won't feel insecure around you. We are all meant to shine, as children do. We were born to make manifest the glory of God that is within us. It's not just in some of us; it's in everyone. And as we let our own light shine, we unconsciously give other people permission to do the same. As we are liberated from our own fear, our presence automatically liberates others."

I love the last line. "When we are liberated from our own fear." When we get out of our own way and are real, "our presence automatically liberates others."

If you want to do more than communicate, if you really want to connect, then get personal.

I don't mean we should share things that people don't want to know or don't need to hear. There are some things that are better left unsaid.

Instead, I'm suggesting that you take your relationships beyond professional. Make them personal. People who are interested take the relationship deeper. Get to know the other person for who they are. What drives them? What excites them? What are their likes and dislikes? What are their hobbies? Their kids' names? When is their birthday or anniversary? What is their favorite restaurant? Their favorite food? Their favorite sports team? What are their dreams? What clubs or associations are they involved in? What accomplishments are they most proud of? (I think you get the point)

If you knew all of these things, would your connection with that person be stronger? Of course it would. Your influence would increase and if this was a client, you would probably end up doing more business with him or her as well.

PRACTICE THE PLATINUM RULE

Chapter 6

PRACTICE THE PLATINUM RULE

> "What's good for the goose isn't always good for the gander."
> – Famous Fable

My daughter Andie is great with people. She is outgoing, personable, caring and has a huge heart. (She is just like her mother) Andie came home from church recently and said, "Dad, do you know what the Golden Rule is?" She was excited over what she had learned, so I asked, "Can you tell me what it is?" She said, "you are supposed to be nice if you want people to be nice." I said, "That's true, treat other people the way that you want to be treated – right?" She said, "Ya, that's the Golden Rule."

sure, as kids, we could all relate to an experience like this, a lesson from a teacher, parent or in church, where the Golden Rule was taught:

Treat Other People The Way You Want To Be Treated.

The Golden Rule appeared over 3000 years ago and is a moral code that is found in virtually all the major religions of the world. The interesting thing about the golden rule is it's perfect for values, but not for communication.

Tony Allesandra said this about The Golden Rule.

"That's an old and honorable sentiment. A lot of good has been done in the world by people practicing The Golden Rule. As a guide to personal values, it can be a powerful force for honesty and compassion. But as a yardstick for communication, The Golden Rule has a downside.

"If applied verbatim, it can backfire and actually cause personality conflicts. Why? Because following The Golden Rule literally – treating other people the way you'd like to be treated – means dealing with others from your own perspective. It implies that we're all alike; that what I want and need is exactly what you want and need. But of course we're not all alike. And treating others that way can mean turning off those who have different needs, desires, and hopes."

That is why when it comes to dealing with people, communication and influence; we need to move beyond The Golden Rule to The Platinum Rule. Treat Other People The Way They Want To Be Treated

The difference is subtle, but in practice it's drastic. It's not about you. It's about them.

APPLYING THE PLATINUM RULE

There are innumerable ways that you can apply the Platinum Rule, ranging from simple to profound, yet every time you treat someone the way they want to be treated, you will leave a lasting impression.

To apply the Platinum Rule efficiently, we need to begin by asking the right questions. A waiter at a Chinese restaurant I visited recently asked the following question as the patrons were seated, "Would you like me to leave a pitcher of water on the table, or would you prefer I fill your glasses throughout the evening?" This simple question allowed the waiter to treat each customer the way they wanted to be treated and I know that as a customer, I appreciated it.

Another great question to ask in today's techno-savvy world pertains to follow-up. There are so many forms of communication that we can use, so I have developed the habit of asking, "What is the best way to follow up with you? Phone? Email? Or Text?" Having this understanding makes my efforts more effective and better received because our communication will be what the person wants, not what I want.

Learning to ask the questions that reveal personal preferences is an essential skill set that you need to develop if you want to apply the platinum rule.

THE FIVE LOVE LANGUAGES

> "What counts in making a happy marriage is not so much how compatible you are, but how you deal with incompatibility."
> – Leo Tolstoy

One of the best books I've ever read on the practical application of The Platinum Rule is called "The Five Love Languages." It has been on the New York Times bestseller list more times than I can count. The book is designed for couples but the information is universal. In the book, the author, Gary Chapman teaches that people receive love in one of five ways. The love languages are:

1) Physical touch
2) Words of Affirmation
3) Quality Time
4) Gifts
5) Acts of Service

The way that you receive love is your love language.

Imagine you are in a relationship and your primary love language is gifts. You love gifts. When someone gives you a gift, you feel validated and know that they care. On the other side, your significant other doesn't care for gifts, but cherishes quality time.

It doesn't do you any good to treat him or her the way that you want to be treated because they receive love differently than you do. A gift does not have the same meaning to them as it does to you. If you really want to connect, you need to treat them the way that they want to be treated and give them uninterrupted, quality time.

This is the platinum rule of relationships at it's finest: Treat other people the way they want to be treated. In personal relationships, business situations and leadership roles, the platinum rule will help you to create influence by placing other people's interests first.

REAL WORLD APPLICATION

To the cynic, The Platinum Rule sounds great in theory but seems too naïve to really work. I can hear them now:

- "If you treat your people the way they want to be treated, then you are going to be giving in to selfish,

inappropriate and unrealistic wants and desires."
- "Most people have a 'me-first' attitude – so you are saying to indulge them?"
- "So the Platinum Rule means to give in, always say yes, and encourage whatever people want. That is a recipe for disaster!"

The Platinum Rule does not mean to indulge unrighteous desires, encourage mediocrity and insubordination, or to be a pushover who always gives in. The Platinum rule means that as a leader you care enough about the individual to treat them as an individual. It is that extra ingredient that leaders can use in a myriad of ways to build bridges with their people and make them feel valued. It is leading through their eyes, understanding their perspective, and helping them achieve their goals. Leadership is never about you. It is always about them.

John Maxwell, when talking about the development of people in leadership said, "I am more successful when I:

- Listen well enough to lead through their eyes.
- Relate well enough to communicate with their hearts.
- Work well enough to place tools in their hands.
- Think well enough to challenge and expand their minds."

Working with thousands of people in a leadership role, I have realized through experience that people respond differently. What drives one person doesn't necessarily drive another.

Some people respond to praise. They want to feel appreciated and validated. Recognition and words of affirmation are felt deeply. As a leader, I always try to give praise that is GPS: genuine, personal and specific. And whenever appropriate, praise publicly.

Other people respond to a challenge. I am this way. I like the opportunity to step up, to grow and to prove myself. I remember a program I was involved in when I was younger. As I was starting the program, my mom sent an email to the director and said, "Ty responds very well to challenge. If you want Ty to give his absolute best, then challenge him." Luckily for me, my mom is a leader who applies The Platinum Rule.

Still others might respond best to financial incentives. I can relate to this kind of shallowness.   If you know this about your people then it doesn't make sense to create a promotion for them, which gives movie tickets, free products or even a trip. If they respond best to money and you want their best effort – that's what you give them.

Some of your people may want an opportunity to lead, a chance to teach, to be heard, to feel trusted, to make a difference, to contribute their ideas in development, and the lists goes on and on. The Platinum Rule is not a naïve approach to leadership; instead it is an engaged, advanced approach.

How well do you know your people? Do you know what drives them? Do you care enough to lead people as individuals and not just as a collective group? Are you willing to put in the time to know how to treat people the way they want to be treated and not the way you want to be treated?

In answer to the cynic – The Platinum Rule is leadership and influence at its finest, because it is the application of care for the individual.

THE POWER OF DIET PEPSI

John Curtis is a person of influence. As the mayor of Provo, Utah, his willingness to invest in the hundreds of city employees is evidenced by his goal to know every employee by name. He's even willing to hand over a pair of movie tickets to any employee whose name he can't remember. John is a great politician who has developed outward thinking. He constantly thinks of others. He even lists his cell phone number on the city website to make himself available to the residents.

Years before John went into politics, he excelled in the business world as a salesman. He spent a large part of his career working for the employee recognition company, OC Tanner. John carried true influence with his clients and brought a tremendous amount of business to the company.

John has always been a hard worker and felt like he would differentiate himself from everyone else by working at times that others tended to slack off. He wanted an edge and was willing to give a little bit more to excel. On Friday afternoons when many sales people take the afternoon off, John was in his office, reaching out to prospective clients.

One of the biggest clients that OC Tanner wanted was the tobacco company, Phillip Morris. One particular Friday afternoon, John called his contact at Phillip Morris who he had spoken to before. She answered the phone and John asked how she was doing. Her response was honest, "I'm hot, tired, and thirsty." She wasn't in much of a mood to talk and the conversation was short. But when they hung up, John remembered a previous conversation in which she told him that she liked Diet Pepsi. John jumped into action.

Her office was 30 minutes away, so he went to a nearby grocery store, bought a cooler, ice and a six-pack of Diet Pepsi and headed to Phillip Morris. When he arrived, his contact at Phillip Morris couldn't believe her eyes.

John understood the platinum rule and treated a client the way that she wanted to be treated. The experience served as a major relationship opener, one they still talk about years later, and Phillip Morris went on to do millions of dollars in business with OC Tanner, thanks to the influential John Curtis.

SEEK TO SERVE

Chapter 7

SEEK TO SERVE

> "Do something for somebody every day for which you do not get paid."
> – Albert Schweitzer

When I decided to pursue professional speaking I had a chance to go to lunch with world-renowned speaker Les Brown. Les was named as one of the Top Five Outstanding Speakers by Toastmasters International. He's been a keynote speaker for audiences as big as 80,000 people, including Fortune 500 companies and organizations all over the world.

As we ate lunch, he graciously entertained and enlightened me with story after story about his speaking career and I learned a lot through his experience. But one piece of advice stood out above all the rest. It's something I've never forgotten. That advice was to never let my own agenda get in the way of what the audience needs to hear. It would not be the first time I'd hear that.

I read a lot of personal development books, In fact in the last 10 years I've read thousands and people often ask me what my favorite book is. I have a hard time deciding on just one because I learn new things from all of them. But right at the top of the list would be "The Seven Habits of Highly Effective People" by Dr. Stephen R. Covey. "Seven Habits" was named the No. 1 business book of the 21st century by Time Magazine.

The first time I met Dr. Stephen Covey was at an event he hosted in his home. A mutual friend introduced us by saying, "Stephen, this is Ty Bennett, he's writing a book." Stephen asked me what the name of the book was. I said the, "The Power of Influence" (the book you're reading right now). He asked me a little bit about the subject matter and then he said, "Ty can I give you some advice?" I'm not very good with math, but his book has sold about 26 million copies and that seemed liked a lot to me, so I said, "I would love your advice."

He said, "Make sure you write your book for the reader and not the writer." I asked, "What do you mean by that?" He said, "A book that's written for the writer, to build him up, to make him successful, will never achieve what it desires. A book that's written for the reader, to teach, to inspire, to help people, will be a homerun." He continued, "it's much more about contribution than achievement." I asked, "But isn't achievement a good thing?" He said, "Actually, life is about contribution and when you really learn how to contribute, you'll achieve all you've ever wanted."

What Stephen Covey taught me about writing a book is the same lesson that Les Brown taught me about being a speaker:

If you want to succeed, serve. Service is Love in Action – It shows concern, care and compassion.

> "A life isn't significant except for it's impact on others' lives."
> – Jackie Robinson

The more we serve our customers, our employees, our neighbors, our family, our friends, the more love we show and the more impact we make.

If we change our approach from what do I get to what can I give, from what can I take out to what can I put in, it makes all the difference.

The more we approach our relationships, our business, our life, with the commitment of providing service to those around us – the more we will get in return.

I believe what Claude M Bristol said in "The Magic of Belief," "Always try to do something for the other fellow and you will be agreeably surprised how things come your way -- how many pleasing things are done for you."

OUTWARD THINKING IN ACTION

When our family put together our family purpose, we discussed our values, passions, and talents. My wife and I both felt a strong desire to put a priority on serving others, to reach out, to help, and to uplift. We added to our purpose statement a motto: Serve God, Serve Each Other, Serve Others. To reinforce this motto, every night before we go to bed, we each share how we helped or served somebody that day. Our four-year-old daughter Andie loves this part, and thinks about it during the day – always making note of opportunities to serve.

For two years I lived in Portugal serving a mission for my church. I remember vividly the day I arrived in Portugal. I didn't speak the language, so I felt lost. Everything was new: exciting but different. I was a long way from America and the comfortable surroundings I was used to. I moved into an apartment where I was assigned. My roommate was Portuguese and spoke very little English.

The next morning I woke up early. My body clock was definitely confused and I sat there in the quiet morning in a blur trying to take in my surroundings. When I looked out the window the view was something I had never seen before. I wasn't used to being in the city, living in an apartment. The road out front was cobblestone, something completely unfamiliar and foreign.

Then I took a shower. When I came out my bed was made and my Doc Martin shoes were sitting nicely at the foot of my bed, freshly polished. My roommate who could not communicate with me in words communicated through service. In an instant, my fears and feelings of isolation disappeared.

One of my favorite passages in any book, comes from Og Mandino's classic, "The Greatest Salesman In The World:"

"I will greet this day with love in my heart. For this is the greatest secret of success in all ventures. Muscle can split a shield and even destroy life but only the unseen power of love can open the hearts of men and until I master this art I will remain no more than a peddler in the market place. I will make love my greatest weapon and none on whom I call can defend against its force. My reasoning they may counter; my speech they may distrust; my apparel they may disapprove; my face they may reject; and even my bargains may cause them suspicion; yet my love will melt all hearts liken to the sun whose rays soften the coldest day."

3 THINGS SERVICE DOES FOR YOU

Although service is about helping the other person, providing service is truly reciprocal. Here are three ways service also serves the server.

1. Service Makes You Happier

When I was in high school, I decided that our DECA club needed to do something that brought us together and provided service. As we discussed it, one of the girls suggested we provide Christmas for a family who needed it. We all got on board, soliciting donations, money, and food. With a monumental effort, we showed up Christmas Eve at the front door of a tiny home in downtown Denver with three SUV's packed full of Christmas. We had toys, candy and clothes for the four kids, food to fill their pantry, and some money for the parents.

As we brought in the first presents I set them down next to a tiny, modestly decorated Christmas tree. Under the tree there were already two presents. I read the tags and knew that they were not the names of the children in the family. Curious, I asked the father about them, and he said. "They are for two of our neighbors who don't have any money for Christmas." I said, "But you don't have any money for Christmas." He said, "I know, but serving makes us happy, and that makes for a great Christmas."

Serving does make us happy. It brings a smile to your face and warms your heart. It helps you focus on what's right with the world and yourself instead of on what's not right.

2. Service Makes You Healthier

Allan Luks, a longtime director of the national Big Brothers Big Sisters organization and author of "The Healing Power of Doing Good," has spent a lifetime studying the many benefits of what is often referred to as the "helper's high." His findings show that "there is a clear cause-and-effect relationship between helping and good health," and that the following occurs after the performance of a kind act:

- There is a rush of euphoria that involves physical sensations and the release of endorphins, the body's natural painkillers.
- Stress related health problems improve.
- The awareness and intensity of physical pain can decrease.
- The health benefits and sense of well-being persists for hours or even days whenever the helping act is remembered.
- The immune system is strengthened.

A nationwide survey conducted by the organization United Health Care found that 84 percent of people who volunteer their service reported feeling physically healthier and 95 percent reported feeling improved emotional health.

It's healthy to give. It doesn't have to be a huge act, it can be dropping a coin in someone else's expired parking meter, or paying the toll for the guy behind you in line; it can be as simple as telling someone you like their tie or the shoes they're wearing, or dropping off a bundle of no-longer-needed household items at the goodwill store.

Whatever it is, and wherever and whenever it's done, it will spread the unmistakable influence of kindness and it will make you feel better.

3. Service Creates The Aura of Leadership

A study at the University of Kent in southern England was dedicated to figuring out how givers are perceived. Researchers conducted an experiment called a "cooperation game" in which participants were each given a small amount of money and asked to contribute to a common fund.

Next, the researchers doubled the common fund and passed it out equally to members of the group. In this game, the best thing for everyone is to continually reinvest their money and keep doubling the fund. But if you're crafty, rather than cooperate you'll be tempted to hold back some of your money. That means that you get your own money, plus a chunk of everybody else's. As the experiment showed, there are always those people who opt to do so.

Then the researchers conducted a second phase of the experiment in which the participants were separated into teams and asked to elect leaders. They found that 82% of the leaders who were elected were those who had given the most back during the first phase. The study concluded that when people see someone giving, and especially when they see someone giving all that they have, they recognize a leadership quality in that person, even if it's a complete stranger.

If people witness you as a giver, they will see you as a leader. Giving says you are seeking to serve, you are interested in placing other people's interests ahead of your own, you are interested in investing in someone else's world, not just your world. You are practicing the platinum rule.

Service. It is the great paradox of positive self-fulfillment: to get all that you want, give others all that they want.

As the English religious leader John Wesley advised, "Do all the good you can, By all the means you can, In all the ways you can, In all the places you can, At all the times you can, To all the people you can, As long as ever you can."

That counsel was given 300 years ago, but the wisdom is timeless. Now, as then, serving others is the key that will make you happier, healthier – and a person of tremendous influence.

About The Author

More than one million people from 50 countries have learned from Ty Bennett's insights on Leadership, Entrepreneurship and Communication.

When Ty was 21 years old he started a business with his brother Scott, which they built to over $20 million in annual revenue while still in their twenties.

Ty was recently featured in Utah Business' Top 40 Under 40.

As a speaker Ty is a young, fresh voice with a fun, engaging style. Ty has shared the stage with celebrities, world renowned thought leaders and recently with President Bush and President Clinton.

Ty is the author of The Power of Influence as well as the video training program, Facts Tell, Stories Sell. His message is changing lives and reaching people around the world.

Ty lives in Utah with his wife Sarah, daughter Andie, and sons Tanner and Drew.

To learn more about Ty Bennett – visit www.leadershipinc.com